QUIET MOMENTS

for a Busy Mom's Soul

EMILIE BARNES

Artwork by Susie Muise

HARVEST HOUSE PUBLISHERS

EUGENE, OREGON

Quiet Moments for a Busy Mom's Soul

Text Copyright © 2004 by Emilie Barnes
Published by Harvest House Publishers
Eugene, Oregon 97402
www.harvesthousepublishers.com

ISBN 0-7369-1452-8

Portions of this book are excerpted from *Minute Meditations™ for Busy Moms* (Harvest House Publishers, 2002).

All works of art appearing in this book are copyrighted by Susie Muise and licensed by Courtney Davis, Inc., San Francisco, California, and may not be reproduced without permission.

Design and Production by Garborg Design Works, Minneapolis, Minnesota

Unless otherwise indicated, all Scripture quotations are taken from the New American Standard Bible ®, © 1960, 1962, 1963, 1968, 1971, 1972, 1973, 1975, 1977, 1995 by The Lockman Foundation. Used by permission. (www.Lockman.org) Verses marked NIV are taken from the HOLY BIBLE, NEW INTERNATIONAL VERSION®. NIV®. Copyright © 1973, 1978, 1984 by the International Bible Society. Used by permission of Zondervan. All rights reserved. Verses marked NKJV are taken from the New King James Version. Copyright © 1982 by Thomas Nelson, Inc. Used by permission. All rights reserved. Verses marked KJV are taken from the King James Version of the Bible.

Printed in China

06 07 08 09 10 11 12 13 / LP / 10 9 8 7 6 5 4 3 2

Contents

Encouragement

And we know that all things work together for good to them that love God, to them who are the called according to his purpose.

Romans 8:28 KJV

It is the sweet, simple things of life which are the real ones after all.

Laura Ingalls Wilder

My purpose is that they may be encouraged in heart and united in love, so that they may have the full riches of complete understanding, in order that they may know the mystery of God, namely, Christ, in whom are hidden all the treasures of wisdom and knowledge.

Colossians 2:2-4

A mother's love for her child is like nothing else in the world.

Agatha Christie

I dwell in possibility.

Emily Dickinson

5

Making Your House a Home

Unless the LORD builds the house, they labor in vain who build it; unless the LORD guards the city, the watchman keeps awake in vain.

Psalm 127:1

As busy moms, we sometimes wonder if we actually have a home—or is it merely a stopover place to eat, do laundry, hang around, and sleep? Or is it just a place to repair things, mow the lawn, paint, wallpaper, and install new carpet? A true home is much more than all that. It's a place of people living together, growing, laughing, crying, learning, and creating together.

A small child, after watching his house burn

down, was quoted as saying, "We still have a
home. We just don't have a house to put it
in." How perceptive of that child.

Our home should be a trauma
center for the whole family. We
don't have to be perfect at home—
just forgiven and forgiving. We can
grow, we can make mistakes, we
can shout for joy, we can cry, we
can agree, and we can disagree.
Home is a place where happy experiences occur. It's a shelter from the
problems of the world, a place
where love happens, acceptance is
given, and security provided.

Father God,
through Your
inspiration and
guidance I turn
our house into a
home. It's so cozy,
warm, comfort-
able, loving, and
such a wonderful
place for rest.
Thanks for helping
to shape this
dwelling. Amen.

Home offers a respite from the
tragedies that seem to plague the
world outside our door, as recounted
on the newscasts. Within our four
walls we can offer a place of peace.

What can we do as moms to
have a home like God intended? As with everything in life,
when something is broken we go back to the instruction man-
ual—in our case, the Bible.

The home is God's invention. He designed the home to be
the foundation of our society, a place to meet the mental,
spiritual, physical, and emotional needs of people. The members of a family must work together to make their home a
true home—not just a place where they hang out.

John Henry Jowett says, "The Bible does not say very
much about homes; it says a great deal about the things that
make them. It speaks about life and love and joy and peace
and rest. If we get a house and put these into it, we shall have
secured a home."

lotion

Our
Baby

susie muise

The Blankie

Peace I leave with you; My peace I give to you; not as the world gives do I give to you. Do not let your heart be troubled, nor let it be fearful.

John 14:27

When our first grandchild was born, her parents named her Christine Marie—Christine from her mother's middle name and Marie from my middle name. I'm very proud of my namesake Christine Marie. She is our only granddaughter among four grandsons.

From flannel fabric I made her a piece of pink-printed blanket with some small roses. The blanket was edged with a pink satin binding. It was only about eight inches by eight inches, very small. Well, it quickly became her security blankie while she sucked her thumb. The blankie got twisted, wadded up, and smoothed by little Christine Marie. She was finally able to pull loose an end and twist the threads around her fingers.

Christine loved her pink rosebud blankie. It gave her comfort when she wasn't feeling well, softness when she was afraid, and security when she felt alone. Then one day five years later the blankie got folded and put in an envelope that she tucked away in her dresser drawer. From time to time she still pulls out the envelope to look at the rosebud

God, thank You for letting me put away my old childhood security blanket and for giving me faith to trust You in all situations. Let me, by example, lead my family to do the same. Amen.

flannel security blanket.

Jesus is like the security blanket that Christine Marie once held close to her. As today's Scripture states, He gives us peace in the midst of the storms of life; when we are going through that difficult tornado of a broken marriage, the death of a dream, financial troubles, ill health, or all the other trials we encounter in just living out our daily lives.

Christ is our security blanket when we are afraid and feel fearful of tomorrow.

My mama used to tell me in the middle of the night when I needed to go to the bathroom but was afraid of the dark, "Be afraid, but go anyway." Today I know I can go because I have my Lord who is with me wherever I go. When I'm weak and upset, He holds me and comforts my heart.

Of course, Jesus is more than just a security blanket. He's our Comforter, our Savior, the Messiah, the Alpha and Omega, the Almighty, the Everlasting, our bright and morning star, our Counselor, our strength, our Redeemer, our peace, our High Priest, our cornerstone, our foundation, our master builder, and a hundred other necessities for us.

It's time to give our blanket over to Jesus and allow Him to be our Master Comforter.

Help Wanted

A cord of three strands is not quickly torn apart.
Ecclesiastes 4:12

Many times we look to others to help us out, and we complain when we don't receive the help we think we deserve. However, help starts from within ourselves *first*, then comes from outside.

I know, as a busy mom, I often had to depend on myself to get something done. Often there was no one around to help during the hectic schedule of a busy day. Perhaps your life is like that too. Take heart—you will get everything done that needs to be done.

At such times, it helps to take an inventory of all the skills and tools God has so graciously given us at birth. We tend to take for granted these attributes for success that were given to us at the very beginning of our lives—our eight fingers and two thumbs.

And although we need to dig in and do our own work, sometimes we *do* need the help of others. King Solomon in all his wisdom tells us that friends are great blessings to us. He says in Ecclesiastes 4:

Two are better than one because they have a good

return for their labor.

...But woe to the one who falls when there is not another to lift him up.

...if two lie down together they keep warm.... ...if one can overpower him who is alone, two can resist him.

A cord of three strands is not quickly torn apart.

Are you working on relationships that build these friendly blessings?

Begin at home with your family members. Throughout Scripture we are reminded to be united, be of the same spirit, be of one accord. Unity should be our goal: wife to husband, parents to children, children to siblings, friend to friend. Your church should be a source of help too. How well do you know the other mothers in your church? Have you reached out to offer help to another mother when she needs it? A good family church is a great place from which to build a network of moms who can help each other through the rough times of motherhood.

Lord, let me fully realize the gift of my ten fingers that You have given me. May I also be appreciative of the other friends You have given me. Help me to be available to serve other mothers as I wish to be helped. Amen.

12

Faith Is a Gift

Now faith is the assurance of things hoped for,
the conviction of things not seen.

Hebrews 11:1

Do you ever have trouble believing in something you haven't seen? The disciple Thomas did. He couldn't bring himself to believe in Jesus' resurrection until he actually saw and touched Jesus.

Jesus told Thomas, "Because you have seen me, you have believed; blessed are those who have not seen and yet have believed" (John 20:29 NIV). I don't believe Jesus was scolding Thomas when He said these words. He was just saying that Thomas would be a lot happier—that's what "blessed" means!—if he could learn to take some things on faith!

I think that's true for us moms too. Every day I take it

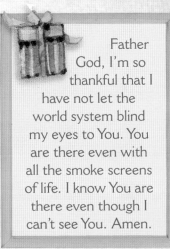

Father God, I'm so thankful that I have not let the world system blind my eyes to You. You are there even with all the smoke screens of life. I know You are there even though I can't see You. Amen.

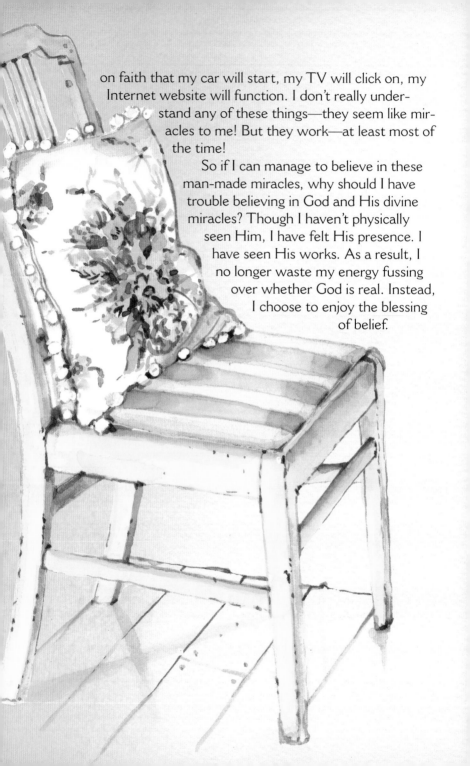

on faith that my car will start, my TV will click on, my Internet website will function. I don't really understand any of these things—they seem like miracles to me! But they work—at least most of the time!

So if I can manage to believe in these man-made miracles, why should I have trouble believing in God and His divine miracles? Though I haven't physically seen Him, I have felt His presence. I have seen His works. As a result, I no longer waste my energy fussing over whether God is real. Instead, I choose to enjoy the blessing of belief.

Behold, Your Mother

Then He said to the disciple, "Behold, your mother!"
John 19:27

*B*eholding one's mother is one of the greatest honors one could bestow on a woman. I realize there are some readers who have not had pleasant experiences with their mothers. However, the position of motherhood is one that should be honored. If you had a good mother, praise the Lord; if not, then you become the mother that you wished you'd had.

One of my favorite mothers is Sarah Edwards. She was one of the great women in American history. She had a great influence on her family even extending to future generations. Sarah was married to the famous theologian, Jonathan Edwards. The couple were the parents of 11 children. It was the responsibility of Sarah to raise those children, and it was a job she took on with great passion!

At the same time, Sarah maintained a vital, loving relationship in her marriage to Jonathan. How did she do it all? After all, she only had 24 hours in a day, just like us. As a deeply Christian woman, Sarah was a firm, patient mother who treated her children with courtesy and love. She was able to guide her children without angry words or temper outbursts. She had only to speak once and her children obeyed her. They had learned to respect their parents, obey God, and always exhibit good manners.

Sarah is one whom we can respect as an expert manager of her colonial home. She wasn't blessed with all the gadgets we have today. She would have loved our microwave ovens, dishwashers, and vacuum cleaners.

Even with her heavy schedule, Sarah made spending time with her Lord her top priority. This gave her strength to fulfill her daily "to-do" list. The Edwards' descendants included:

God, give me a mentor from whom I can learn. Modeling is so very important. I'm looking for a good road map. Please send me a godly woman to learn from. Amen.

    13 college presidents
    65 college professors
    100 lawyers
    30 judges
    66 physicians
    80 holders of public office
    3 U.S. senators
    3 mayors of large cities
    3 state governors
    1 vice president of the United States
    1 comptroller of the U.S. Treasury Department

All Sarah's work as a mother paid great dividends. Her descendants would truly rise up and call her blessed. I wonder, will ours?

The Lost Mitt

And the LORD will continually guide you,
and satisfy your desire in scorched places,
and give strength to your bones;
and you will be like…a spring of water
whose waters do not fail.

Isaiah 58:11

It was my son Brad's first real leather baseball mitt. My husband Bob had taught him how to break it in with special oil to form the pocket just right for catching the ball. Brad loved his mitt and worked for hours each day to make it fit just right. He was so happy to have such a special glove for his games and practices.

One afternoon after practice, one of the older boys asked to see Brad's mitt. He looked it over, then tossed it away into the grassy field. Brad ran to find his special possession, but he couldn't find it. Nowhere was his mitt to be found. With a frightened, hurt heart,

Brad came home in tears.

I encouraged him by saying that the mitt is there someplace and let's go look. "But Mom, I did search the lot, and it's not there," replied Brad, in tears.

So I said, "Brad, let's pray and ask God to help us." By now it was beginning to get dark and we needed to hurry, so we jumped into the car. As I drove to the baseball field, we asked God to please guide our steps directly to the exact spot where the glove was. After parking, we quickly headed for the field. Again we asked God to point us in the right direction. Brad ran into the tall grass and, about 20 feet away, was Brad's glove.

Lord, what an encourage-ment to me that You care about the smallest details of my life. I do want to be a spring of water to those around me. Amen.

God answers our prayers. Sometimes it's "wait," "yes," or "later." For Brad that day it was a yes. God said in essence, "I'll direct you to find the mitt of this young boy whose heart was broken because of a bully and a lost glove."

Do you have a "lost glove" today? Go before God and praise Him for the promise He gave us in Isaiah 58:11. If God says it, believe it. He will direct you and guide you. Open your heart to listen to what His direction is, then press ahead. The grass may seem too tall for you to see very far, but trust the Lord and keep walking until you feel in your heart the peace you desire. God may lead in a direction you least expect, but step forward with confidence in the Lord.

Giving Strength When Weak

He gives strength to the weary, and to him
who lacks might He increases power.
Isaiah 40:29

*A*re you always tired? As a busy mom, I yearned for rest and sleep. The activities of the day often seemed beyond my strength. At no time in my life can I remember ever being so utterly drained of energy. Each day I looked forward to evening when I could tuck the children into bed and get some well-needed rest.

I'm sure those days weren't much fun for Bob either. When he came home from work, my energy had long since been sapped by the day's activities. By age 21, I was responsible for five children—our two and my brother's three children whom Bob and I took in. Life at that time absolutely overwhelmed me.

At such times of low physical reserves, we are open prey for the enemy. Satan can attack us with all sorts of accusations

> Lord, my Strength, when I feel weak, let me rely on Your strength. I will not let Satan take advantage of my tiredness. Instead I turn to You and receive the victory set aside for me in Christ.
> Amen.

about our lot in life. His goal is to cause us to resent the demands made on us and to cast doubt on God's faithfulness.

But God knows our weaknesses and in every case will send the strength we need for every day's circumstances. No more, no less. Just enough.

Mom, don't be discouraged by your weaknesses. God knows your need. He really does. It's human to be tired after a mom's full day, but how we handle our tiredness is of utmost importance. Our power for living *must* depend on faith in the source of our power—Jesus Christ.

During times of extreme stress, look fully to His great promise that He gives power to the weak and He increases strength to those who have no might. Claim this as your "tired promise." Do it as often as necessary—*even if it's every day!*

Moments of Res

nd Renewal

Find out for yourself the form of rest that refreshes you best.

Daniel Considine

Take rest; a field that has rested gives a bountiful crop.

Ovid

Create in me a pure heart, O God, and renew a steadfast spirit within me.

Psalm 51:10

Sit in reverie, and watch the changing color of the waves that break upon the idle seashore of the mind.

Henry Wadsworth Longfellow

When I slow down long enough to smell the roses, I usually see the beauty and all else that is ours to share.

Morgan Jennings

Good News Before Bad News

All Scripture is inspired by God and profitable
for teaching, for reproof, for correction, for training in
righteousness; so that the man of God may be adequate,
equipped for every good work.

2 Timothy 3:16-17

Some days I wake up and reach for the morning paper or turn on the radio to catch the latest news. After all, it's important to be well informed about world events. But after a few short days of this, I'm reminded of a saying that I once heard: *Read the Good News before you read the bad news.*

That's absolutely right. Why would any busy mother, already carrying the important responsibilities of her family, want to start the day off with the bad

Father God, I pray for the energy and discipline it will take to commit to time with You each day. It is what I long for…please, gently urge my spirit to enter Your presence. I want to draw from the Source of Good News before I face the busy day. Grow my passion for this daily activity, Lord.
Amen.

news that always seems to make the biggest headlines before she reads the Good News of Scripture?

Over the years I've made it a point to start off each day by reading and thinking about God's Word. When the children were young, I set the alarm 30 minutes before the rest of the family's wake-up call so I could start the day off right. This practice seemed to energize my day as a mother and set me heading in the right direction. On days when I skipped my time with the Lord, I often encountered frustration and lack of focus. I seemed to move along from one small crisis to the next, without the peace that only comes as a result of time spent alone with God.

Restoration

*He restores my soul; He guides me in
the paths of righteousness....*
Psalm 23:3

Princess Elizabeth, daughter of Charles I, was found dead
one day with her head leaning on the Bible and the Bible
open at the words, "Come unto me all ye that labor and are
heavy laden, and I will give you rest." Her monument in
Newport Church consists of a female figure reclining her head
on a marble book, with the above text engraved on the book.

As busy moms you can relate to the notion that you need
rest. We are wearing thin mentally, physically, and emotionally
by all that we must do. We seem to be running in circles just to
keep up with our hectic schedules. Faster, faster, and still we get
behind.

How does one get restored? Listen to this wise advice:
• You don't have to be a super mom.
• You don't have to be perfect.
• Accept limitations on what you can do.
• Meet God each day in study and prayer.
• Say "No" to good things and save your "Yes"
  for the best.
• Enjoy the small wonders around you.
• God restores you.

Father God, You can and do restore my soul. Only through You can I restore my soul. You are my resting place. Amen.

And It Was Good

And God saw that it was good.
Genesis 1:10

*A*s moms on the go, we often don't take the time to see, hear, and smell God's creation. We find ourselves being so busy that we don't take the precious time to study God's creation in its fullness.

Do you see evidence of God when you look around you? As I'm writing, the day is foggy where I live, and I can spy a single drop of dew on the leaves out my kitchen window. With the sun breaking through the fog bank, this little drop of moisture is giving back to God a tiny sparkle of light that He sent from heaven.

Shakespeare spoke of "a gentle dew from heaven." He too must have taken a pause to look at a droplet of God's creation. He too must have been moved by

> God, it is so good just to know that You created the droplets left by fog, so good to know You care about the smallest elements of life. Amen.

the wonder of even such a small sample of God's work.
I can fully understand how God, after His work of creation, looked it over and con-
firmed that it was good. If only we
humans, after we create something, could be as satisfied with
our work before we move on to
another activity or project.

If only we were more concerned
about the quality of our work.
Our culture hungers for excellence. As moms, let's rest
between creations. Slow
down and wait until the
Lord tells us "it is good."

Knowing God in Stillness

Be still, and know that I am God.
Psalm 46:10 NKJV

We are a culture that is severely overstimulated. There's loud music at home, the mall, and even at most restaurants. Advertisements fill everything we read, hear, and see. No wonder we live in an era where people have short attention spans, hearing problems, and a difficult time being still.

Do we even bother to listen for stillness, quietness, and silence anymore?

Yes, each of these do have a sound and it is so refreshing. For some people who have become addicted to noise, these sounds are uncomfortable. They become uneasy, nervous, twitching; they need sounds—loud sounds.

But quiet times are refreshing to the soul, offering

God of Peace, help me establish a quiet time each day so I can be still. In this stillness let me ponder who You are and may I know You in a greater way. Help me to establish my home as a place of peace. Amen.

us reflection, perhaps a chance to mourn or to be happy or maybe even to hear God speak to us in a still, small voice.

Do such times exist in your home? Or is your house filled with the discordant sounds of television and pop music? Is it any wonder then that you and your children don't know how to cultivate silence?

Perhaps your children are already well on the road to the addiction to noise—the need for constant audio activity. If so, you will be shortchanging them by not teaching them the joys of pure silence.

The psalmist knew that in order to know God we have to stop striving and become still. The busy-ness of life must come to a halt in order to know God. When we find ourselves with a hectic schedule and we're not sure we can get everything done, that is the moment to call "time-out" and seek the quietness that God can give us. Even a stillness of 60 to 90 seconds can restore your sense of direction. It doesn't take long.

A Time for Everything

He hath made every thing beautiful in his time.
Ecclesiastes 3:11 KJV

Ralph Waldo Emerson said it so well:

> *Finish every day and be done with it. You have done what you could. Some blunders and absurdities no doubt crept in; forget them as soon as you can. Tomorrow is a new day; begin it well and serenely and with too high a spirit to be cumbered with old nonsense. This day is all that is good and fair. It is too dear, with its hopes and invitations, to waste a moment on yesterday.*

Lord of Time and Life, You are the Alpha and the Omega. You are the beginning and the end. Help me be patient and learn to live at peace with Your timetable. Let me not rush my agenda. Let me trust You more. Amen.

Truly there is a season for everything. Behind every happening, there is a purpose. Nothing happens by accident. Life flows through its natural cycles. There is a time to be born, a beginning, and a

time to die, an ending. God has a divine timetable.

My mother-in-law recently passed away, and we were richly blessed by knowing that her cycle of life on earth had been completed as God has planned. We knew that through the years, God had turned every ugly event in her life beautiful. And now she was trading her earthly life for one in which there is no more pain.

During her life she had heartaches and laughter, along with sickness and health. There were no "whys" when she passed away. We knew that it was all part of God's cycle for her. When we realize that God has a timing for everything, then we can trust that everything will be beautiful in His perfect time.

Thankfulness

Fortunate are the people whose roots are deep.

Agnes Meyer

Gratitude takes nothing for granted; is never unresponsive, is constantly awakening to new wonder, and to praise of the goodness of God.

Thomas Merton

The best and most beautiful things in the world cannot be seen or even touched. They must be felt with the heart.

Helen Keller

Abundance is, in large part, an attitude.

Sue Patton Thoele

Every good and perfect gift is from above, coming down from the Father of the heavenly lights, who does not change like shifting shadows.

James 1:17

In Everything, Not for Everything

*In everything give thanks; for this is the will
of God in Christ Jesus for you.*
1 Thessalonians 5:18 NKJV

*L*ast evening we received two telephone calls that really
test this verse. One was regarding a 15-year-old boy who
had just been hospitalized to begin a grueling chemotherapy
regimen to combat his newly diagnosed cancer.

The next call was regarding a
mother who went in for a midlife
hysterectomy. The doctors, in
performing a routine biopsy,
discovered cervical cancer.

How do we say
"Thank You, God" for
tragedies and sudden
crises that threaten to
destroy our world? I
struggled with this ques-
tion until I realized that
this passage says, "*in* everything," not "*for* everything."

"In everything" is not the

same as "for everything." We don't give thanks for evil or for its tragic results. And at some time or another, we all come face-to-face with evil or an unexpected crisis that threatens us or our family. At such times, no mother can be thankful for the evil that threatens her loved ones, but she can and must be thankful to the God who oversees all that comes our way.

> Father God, may Your will be done in my life. Today and every day. Help me give thanks "in everything." Help me to look closely to see the good in all that You do. Amen.

Even in the midst of our pain, God is always at work. We can remain grateful throughout our ordeal because we live in Jesus Christ and because we know that God cares for us even more than we care for our own children. God is the only perfect parent—and in Him, we find refuge in the day of trouble. Through every circumstance that comes our way, God continues to transform us into the image of His Son.

Matthew Henry, the well-known Bible commentator, made the following entry in his diary after he had been robbed:

> Let me be thankful—first, because I was never robbed before; second, because although they took my wallet, they did not take my life; third, because although they took my all, it was not much; and fourth, because it was I who was robbed, not I who robbed.

Here is a man who knew how to make lemonade out of a lemon. Here is a man who could give thanks *in* everything.

The art of successful living is to seek out thankfulness in all of life's events—to see meaning in every challenge and trust that God will work every adversity to our ultimate good.

How to Love the Rich Life

For the sun rises with a scorching wind
and withers the grass;
and its flower falls off and the beauty
of its appearance is destroyed;
so too the rich man in the midst
of his pursuits will fade away.

James 1:11

One of our young grandchildren asked Papa Bob, "Are you rich?"

"Yes, in the Lord," he answered.

"No, Papa, I mean *really* rich?" he insisted. He wanted to know if his grandpa was *monetarily* rich. The good old capitalist word: money.

Regardless of where most of us are on the financial barometer of life, we are rich compared to someone—especially when we consider the world's population. Just by living in America we are rich. If you don't think so, just ask any of the many immigrants, legal and illegal, who come to this country every year.

And being rich carries a lot of responsibility. When one is wealthy, that person usually has power over things and people. In

38

God, You are a provider of abundance. May our family be found worthy to be a steward of all Your resources. I thank You for the riches You have given us. Amen.

1 Timothy 6:10 we read, "For the love of money is a root of all sorts of evil, and some by longing for it have wandered away from the faith and pierced themselves with many griefs."

The writer isn't saying that being rich is wrong, but that the love of money is the basis for all kinds of evil. We need to examine our attitude toward material wealth. And the result of that examination should determine how we live—because how we live communicates what our concept of wealth is to our children.

A simple lifestyle (as opposed to an ostentatious, wasteful lifestyle) lets our children know that whatever riches we have aren't the most important priority in our life. Instead, let's be good stewards of the gifts God has given us—giving generously to others in need, both of our time and our financial resources. And bring your children into discussions about how and where to give to others.

Show your kids that your security and peace don't come from your bank account but from your relationship with God. Live in such a way that your children will understand that your riches in heaven are more exciting than your riches on earth. Teach them that it's more blessed to give than to receive.

Pray While They're Young

He has given heed to the voice of my prayer.
Psalm 66:19

Depending on how old your children are, you will soon learn the power of prayer, if you haven't already.

As my children got older, my prayer life became stronger. Somehow children bring parents to their knees—especially as those children go through their teen years. During these awkward years there are so many things that we can't control. Cutting the "apron strings" is very difficult, particularly for us moms.

Somehow dads seem to handle these times a lot better. I remember how cool my Bob would stay during very difficult situations. I often commented under my breath that for him to maintain such composure, he surely must not understand the problem.

When those little "bundles of joy" were

> God, thank You for [each child's name]. I love this wonderful human being You have given me to mother. Remind me daily to keep my children bathed in prayer. Help me be the exact mother they need. Amen.

40

young, they were so much fun—but as
teenagers, they turned into reasons
to pray.

   Don't wait until they're older
to pray diligently for your children.
Every day ask God to guide them,
draw them to Him, and
keep them safe.

Bless Your Spouse

So then we pursue the things which make for peace and the building up of one another.

Romans 14:19

You would think that "blessing your spouse" would be very easy to do, but my observation is that sometimes it's hard. Marriage partners have to work together to be at peace and to build up one another.

The word "blessing" comes from two Greek words meaning "well" and "word." When you bless your husband, you're literally saying, "I speak well of my spouse."

We bless our mates when we speak well of them, compliment them, and encourage them. That goes for our children also.

Father God, let me be a blessing to my husband and to my children. I want my spouse to know that I love him and he is my priority for our marriage. I want my children to indeed be blessed. Help me as I try daily to bless them. Amen.

Here are some good ways to develop the habit of blessing your mate:

1. Make a decision never to be critical of your partner's thoughts, words, or deeds.
2. Observe what makes him tick. Be creative in how you relate to his ticker.
3. List your husband's positive traits. Think on these. Give his negative qualities to God.
4. Make it a habit to be positive in your comments. Lift him up in private and in public.
5. Let your husband know for sure that you are on the same team as he is. Let him know that you are his biggest fan and his number-one supporter.

Today Is a Gift

We were burdened excessively, beyond our strength,
so that we despaired even of life.

2 Corinthians 1:8

*D*oes that Scripture sound like your life? Well, maybe not quite "despairing of life," I hope. But your complex role as a busy mom is almost beyond description. Without a doubt you have one of the most difficult, demanding, and taxing job descriptions in the world.

When I'm out and about shopping, I see you younger moms with your children, and I quickly think back to the day when Bob and I had five children in our home. I remember how tired I was—always! I never seemed to get enough rest.

Today the ever-increasing pressures and stresses of living are even faster paced, making it almost impossible for us to live the abundant life we all seek. While striving for excellence at work, Dad must also be a loving husband, father, and leader of his family. Meanwhile, you as Mom have your stresses regarding the

44

management of your household—keeping the children focused, satisfying your husband, and maintaining a proper balance in your life. What a recipe for stress!

But as believers we can endure these stresses successfully if we view life's pressures as opportunities for us to demonstrate God's power. The following poem, which appeared in an old publication, *Record of Faith*, makes that point:

Pressed out of measure and pressed to all length;
Pressed so intensely, it seems beyond strength;
Pressed in the body, and pressed in the soul;
Pressed in the mind till the dark surges roll.
Pressured by foes, and pressure from friends,
Pressed into knowing no helper but God;
Pressed into loving the staff and the rod;
Pressed into living a life in the Lord;
Pressed into living a Christ-life outpoured.
Author Unknown

How we respond to our various pressures helps shape us into the person we will be tomorrow. If it takes all these stresses to make us into the person God has designed us to be, then all these uncomfortable situations will have made it all worthwhile.

Consider that your job as a mom is also God's means for revealing His strength as you tackle the duties you face daily. With each inconvenience you meet, may you realize that this too is merely a building block for whom God wants you to become.

Father, no one enjoys the pressures of life, but if I look at them as teaching tools for whom I am becoming, then I say, "Bring it on." Amen.

45

Take Time to Say I Love You

Permit the children to come to Me; do not hinder them;
for the kingdom of God belongs to such as these.
Mark 10:14

In our "on-the-go" lifestyle, we don't often take the time to show love to our children. Time quickly passes by, and before you know it, they're soon too big to sit on your lap and too bashful to let you hug them.

Jesus knew that children were special, and He often used them in His teachings. While you are blessed to have them in your home, take advantage of these years. If you don't, someday later you'll look back and say, "I didn't spend enough time with my children." But today you can begin to ensure that those words will never be necessary.

Don't let a day go by without saying, "I love you." Don't let a day pass without hugging your children. Speak kindly to them every day. Find something to

> Lord, let me take time to be with my children. Help me establish better priorities so I will take the necessary time. I don't want any regrets at the end of the day. Amen.

laugh about with them. Explore with them. Play with them. Be a fun and loving mom.

An unknown (but wise) author says it best:

Dear little child: Today I told you you were too big to cry…too rough with the kitten…too careless with crayons. I told you to share your toys, but I did not share my time. I was too busy to rock you and hum Brahms' "Lullaby"…

Dear middle-sized child: Today I reminded you your hair was too long…your hamster was hungry… and you were spending too much time with "that boy." I said drink your juice…match your socks…and study your spelling. But I had no time to help with the model airplane or look at your bug collection…

Dear teenager: Today I admonished you to keep your voice down and your shoulders up. Why was your bed unmade…your light on late…your phone call long? I said "No" to mascara…the family car…and a school-night party. But I had no time to say you looked neat and that I was glad you made the team…

Dear child-gone-away: Today I sorted the possessions you left…and remembered you owe me a letter…promised pictures…and have not been home for—how long? But it did not occur to me to telephone you even though I enjoy your calls on my special days…

Moments of

This is our purpose: to make as meaningful as possible this life that has been bestowed upon us; to live in such a way that we may be proud of ourselves; to act in such a way that some part of us lives on.

Oswald Spengler

Because your love is better than life, my lips will glorify you. I will praise you as long as I live, and in your name I will lift up my hands. My soul will be satisfied as with the richest of foods; with singing lips my mouth will praise you.

Psalm 63:3-5

Love and the hope of it are not things one can learn; they are a part of life's heritage.

Maria Montessori

Fulfillment

The greatest challenge of the day is: how to bring about a revolution of the heart, a revolution which has to start with each one of us? When we begin to take the lowest places, to wash the feet of others, to love our brothers with that burning love, that passion, which led to the cross, then we can truly say, "Now I have begun."

Dorothy Day

In a realistic, here-and-now sense, my daily, moment-to-moment experience of God is to love and to serve and to give.

Wayne Dyer

Live Life on Purpose

*Whether, then, you eat or drink or whatever you do,
do all to the glory of God.*
1 Corinthians 10:31

Have you ever been challenged to live life on purpose? If not, I so challenge you now. Especially in your life as a mother. God has plans for your children—and for you. It's not His will that we coast through life casually and aimlessly. Life's far too short for that.

God has placed us here on earth for a reason. And when we discover that reason and live our life to that godly end, we find true satisfaction.

In my life I've been fortunate to meet a lot of wonderful people. But the people I count the most successful are those who understand that everything is to be done to the glory of God. They directed their lives toward a purpose—and that simple difference has given them the impetus and energy to

> Creator, give me purposeful direction on living a life that will glorify You. I'm tired of "shooting from the hip"; I'm weary of coasting. Help me choose wisely and move toward the right goals. Amen.

succeed where many others have failed.

In ancient days, all the craftsmen, artisans, and musicians proclaimed their godly purpose in life by what they produced. That's why the great classics of the world reflect a spiritual tribute to who God is. Through their endeavor, their work was beautiful.

In the twenty-first century few artists are creating works that will attain "classic" status. Why? Because most composers, sculptors, writers, and artists don't create their work to glorify God. Just look at most of our contemporary music, art, theater, cinema, and literature to see how we have strayed.

One of your duties as a mom is to watch and pray for your children. What are their talents? How can you help them discover their purpose? How can you encourage them to use their God-given gifts for His glory and not to merely follow the crowd?

God's desire is for you and for each member of your family to be purposeful human beings, to work toward meaningful goals and experience the joy of achievement.

So learn to live your life on purpose, and teach your children to do the same. If necessary, write out some obtainable goals and work toward them. Read books that motivate you toward your goal or that help you set worthy goals. Above all, pray for God's guidance in your "on-purpose" life.

United We Stand

*For this reason a man shall leave his father and his
mother, and be joined to his wife; and they shall
become one flesh.*

Genesis 2:24

*I*n union there is power. A single drop of water by itself
is meaningless. But many single drops united by the
force of attraction will form a stream, and many streams
combined will form a river, until the rivers pour their water
into the mighty oceans whose waves defy the power of
man.

When forces act
independently, they are
utterly without power,
but when acting collec-
tively they have mighty
strength. So it is with a
husband and wife—
particularly in their
parental roles. When a
mom or a dad operates
alone, there is limited
power in the family
unit. But a man and a
woman combined,

Father God, help
me bring unity to
our family. I want
the peace that
comes from harmony
between a man and wife. I
want our children to benefit
from the gifts that a united
mother and father can bring
to the family. Help me in
pursuing this goal. Amen.

each fulfilling their place in the family, makes for incredible strength and security—indispensable in raising healthy children. Disunity between Mom and Dad can result in insecurity and anxiety in children. Don't leave such a legacy to your children.

If we don't stand together as husband and wife, Dad and Mom, letting God make us one in spite of our differences, we will easily be defeated and so will our children. That's one reason why God calls a couple to

Departure (a man will leave his father and mother)
Permanence (cleave, or be joined, to his wife)
Oneness (they shall become one flesh)

Becoming one doesn't mean becoming the same. However, oneness means sharing the same degree of commitment to the Lord, to the marriage, and to the children. Such oneness results when two individuals reflect the same Christ within. Such spiritual unity produces tremendous strength in a marriage and in a family.

For this togetherness to happen, the two marriage partners must leave their families (Mom and Dad) and let God make them one. As women, we help the cleaving process when we show our husbands that they are our most important priority after God.

If you clearly communicate your love to your husband, your marriage relationship will become more dynamic and your children will benefit.

God Knows My Name

I have called you by name; you are Mine!
Isaiah 43:1

Charles Haddon Spurgeon once said, "He who counts the stars, and calls them by their names, is in no danger of forgetting His own children. He knows you as thoroughly as if you were the only creature He ever made, or the only saint He ever loved."

One of the advantages of living in a town for a long time is that people know your name. No matter where you go—to the bank, to church, to school, to the pharmacy, or to the car wash—they all say, "Hello, Mrs. Barnes."

This tells me they care, they have an interest in me—and it also makes for good business. One of my brothers-in-law patronizes a certain restaurant because they greet him by name every time he enters. When he entertains a guest for a meal, he likes the guest to know that the restaurateur knows Mr. Barnes by name.

> Lord of Lords and King of Kings, since I am Yours and You are mine, I want to respect You and Your position. Let my speech approach You accordingly. Amen.

My Bob knows he's in real trouble when I address him with, "Barnes." He then begins to really pay attention.

God knows you by name. He summons you and you are His. How awesome this is to believe. You don't belong to anyone else. You are *His*. That's what makes us all so special; we are God's children. When you address your family members, remember that they too are owned by God—they are His children. Treat them with the respect due God's children.

Being Passed Over

For not from the east, nor from the west,
nor from the desert comes exaltation;
but God is the Judge; He puts down one
and exalts another.
Psalm 75:6-7

Nothing hurts like being passed over in life when you feel like you should have been selected for the team, chosen for the lead in the play, elected president of the club, or perhaps loved by that handsome football player you had a crush on in high school.

Today's verse is for all of us bypassed people who have been left out. We all have wanted a certain position and didn't get it. We all have felt the sting of rejection, and there's perhaps only one thing more painful—watching our children be passed over for something on which they've set their heart.

At such times, Mom is often the one to whom they turn for consolation. You'll be called on to offer a lesson in how to

56

respond to times of disappointment. The wise mother will point her disappointed child to this powerful verse in Psalms.

God will lift up in His time, not ours. This is a hard, but very valuable, life lesson. God knows our hearts and yet is always wise in His decisions. It is someone else's time right now, and it will help your child heal if they learn to rejoice with those who rejoice.

Their day will come and it will be even sweeter for them, knowing that God has chosen the time for them to be picked.

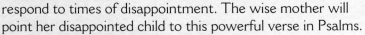

Father God, take from me the desire for earthly recognition. Let me focus on the task, not on the reward. I know that You will lift me up in Your time—I trust You for that. Help me be a supportive mom when the time comes for me to comfort my child when he or she has been passed over. Amen.

Always Means Always

[Love] always protects, always trusts,
always hopes, always perseveres.
1 Corinthians 13:7 NIV

Sometimes it's hard for us mere mortals to understand adequately the word "always." In today's culture we don't understand love as that kind of commitment. When we say "always," don't we usually mean "sometimes"...or "most of the time"? But "always" really means eternal and everlasting. Can we really commit to *always*?

When God through Scripture says "always," it means "always"—no exception. Never changing, dependable for eternity. I am challenged when Paul says that love...

Always protects
Always trusts
Always hopes
Always perseveres

I so want my husband and children to

Almighty, I want to be an "always" person. When I say something, I want it always to be true. My friends can say, "If she said it, it must be true." What a great responsibility to be that kind of woman. Amen.

honor me with that kind of love. I want to be a woman who is known for her word: "When Mom says something, you can take it to the bank." In this regard, my advice to moms is, "Just do what you say you are going to do." By so doing, you teach your children the meaning of being trustworthy. You also teach them to trust others—and that's a rare quality in this age of cynicism. But I've learned that he or she who trusts others will make fewer mistakes than the person who distrusts others.

The Living Bible translates Romans 8:24 into, "We are saved by trusting. And trusting means looking forward to getting something we don't yet have—for a man who already has something doesn't need to hope and trust that he will get it."

Moms, we are to be women of integrity. Our word can *always* be trusted. When we are these kind of women, our husbands, our children, and our friends will stand at the gate and call us blessed.

Every Job Is Significant

Whatever you do, do your work heartily,
as for the Lord rather than for men.
Colossians 3:23

As a burned-out mom, do you get discouraged when no one in the family seems to appreciate all the endless things you do for them? I know I did—until one day I realized I was trying to serve the wrong people. I switched tactics and began to work heartily for the Lord rather than for man. My expectations turned completely around—my goal was to serve and be a witness to those to whom I ministered.

If sometimes your work seems like a waste of time, then maybe you could begin to consider your work (either in or out of the home) as a place of ministry—then perform your duty as if you were doing it for Jesus. He's the One you're really serving.

"Why do I do what I do? Is it to please man or God?" These two questions we must

> God, may I want to serve You rather than man. Let my joy be complete in You! I only need Your praises. Amen.

answer ourselves because how we answer reveals how we look at life. If we work to please people, we will never be satisfied because people always expect more from us, and we can never give enough. If we work to please God, then we will hop out of bed each morning to see what the new day brings.

Perhaps if we take up this challenge, we can profit by listening to John Dodd, who wrote several centuries ago: "Whatsoever our calling be, we serve the Lord Christ in them....They are the most worthy servants...that...serve the Lord, where He hath placed them."

If God's purposes are to be fulfilled, we must not neglect the ordinary tasks in our pursuit of the glorious ones. Meals must be cooked, trash must be collected, assembly lines must be manned, and children must be attended to. Every service done unto God is significant.

Martin Luther once said, "A dairy maiden can milk a cow to the glory of God."

Look Forward, Not Backward

Do not call to mind the former things,
Or ponder things of the past.
Isaiah 43:18

$\mathcal{H}$ave you ever been a prisoner of your past? Have the steel bars of guilt held you captive? Do you break out in sweat when conversation comes out about what you used to be? Do certain triggers set off memories of the life you used to lead?

At one time or another most of us suffer from painful memories of what we were before we knew the Lord. One thing that I like so much about hearing people give their testimonies is how great the grace of God is. He can take the worst of sinners (which we all have been) and make us white as snow. No social programs, as great as they may

> Lord, You know how I want to be like You. The deepest part of my heart and soul aches for Your wisdom. May today and every day to follow be a special day for new revelation. I am excited about the future You have already conceived for me. Move me forward, Lord. Amen.

be, can change and wash a person's past with the purity of forgiveness.

In 2 Corinthians 5:17 Paul says, "Therefore if anyone is in Christ, he is a new creature; the old things passed away; behold, new things have come." The grace of God not only justifies but also makes "a new creation," which results in a changed life.

Only God can move you forward into the future He has planned for you.